Insistence, Persistence, and Resistance

Insistence, Persistence, and Resistance

collected poems by

Lee Orlich Bertram

© 2024 Lee Orlich Bertram Books LLC. All rights reserved.
This material may not be reproduced in any form, published,
reprinted, recorded, performed, broadcast,
rewritten or redistributed without
the explicit permission of Lee Orlich Bertram Books LLC.
All such actions are strictly prohibited by law.

Cover design by Shay Culligan
Cover image by iStockphoto.com/Chayantorn
Author photo by Jennifer Cass

ISBN: 978-1-63980-544-0
Library of Congress Control Number: 2024938989

Kelsay Books
502 South 1040 East, A-119
American Fork, Utah 84003
Kelsaybooks.com

Insistence, Persistence, and Resistance

collected poems by

Lee Orlich Bertram

© 2024 Lee Orlich Bertram Books LLC. All rights reserved.
This material may not be reproduced in any form, published,
reprinted, recorded, performed, broadcast,
rewritten or redistributed without
the explicit permission of Lee Orlich Bertram Books LLC.
All such actions are strictly prohibited by law.

Cover design by Shay Culligan
Cover image by iStockphoto.com/Chayantorn
Author photo by Jennifer Cass

ISBN: 978-1-63980-544-0
Library of Congress Control Number: 2024938989

Kelsay Books
502 South 1040 East, A-119
American Fork, Utah 84003
Kelsaybooks.com

To Jack, my love and best fan

Acknowledgments

During my youth, I often thought about how different my family members were on both sides, as far as mainstream, American families stood. As I matured over the years, however, I grew to appreciate their differences and my heritage. Those humble, industrious German and Yugoslavian people provided me with colorful lenses to view a world textured with opportunities. They inculcated in me a strict work ethic and taught me the importance of education, languages, music and the arts, writing, and books. I stand eternally grateful to them and the images they left behind that have fueled much of my poetry.

Enjoy the read.

Lee Orlich Bertram
Winter 2023

Contents

A Poem Today	13
Seven Instruments and a Volkswagen	14
Whispers for a Future Self	15
Traveling though Jasmine Nights	16
A Toss of the Salad	18
Anxious I Was	20
On the Road, Down the Road, Turn Off the Road	21
To the Quiet Knoll	23
Queen Tiye—Hound of Royalty	25
Insistence, Persistence, and Resistance	27
The Private Scaffold	28
L.P.	29
Mind Leaves	30
Light Sensations	31
Time at its Beginning	32
Life on the Hindenburg	33
Upon Hearing Barack's Words	35
Come, the Ravages	37
Fateful Christmas Tree	38
Waiting for Mr. H	39
Adieu, Blue Flower	40
A Matter of Seconds	41
Discovering Howard Carter	42
Continuance	44
Friendship Rebounds	45
The Adored Microwave	46
Seduction by Darkness	47
Tell Me Your Name	48
Fleeing from Façades	49
Music Courses within Me	50
Flattery Will Get You Nowhere	51
They Called Her Vesna	52
Brilliant Bliss	54

Laughing, I Went in	55
Stepping Past a Dream	56
Faces Full of Waves	57
The Brightest Echo	59
Sky Children of Nature	60
Persistent Love	61
The Flavor of Cold	62
Are We the Dizzy Intruders?	63
An Autumn Reality	64
Elusion	65
Andersch's Cherries of Freedom	66
Effects from Endless Peaches	68
Blue Tunnels	69
Reflections on Heritage	70
Speaking with Eyes	71
Dew on the Slug	72
A Gathering of those Old Sayings	74
Waiting for the Exact Hour	76
Look to the Vastness not Yesterday's Hurt	77
Not Impressed by his French Kiss	78
Where I Rest	80
A Girl on Standby	81
Silent Shroud	82
Winter Anew	83
Rainy Life Tears	84
Angles of Love	85
In Love with Love	86
Fantasy of Fantasies	87
Death of the Top Hat	88
Windows for Choosing	91
Purple Salve	92

A Poem Today

Perhaps, I will write a poem today.
One poem will do,
I know.

I want to write a poem today.
Any poem will do,
I hope.

Come to me today, my poem.
I will wait for you,
with kind words.

Seven Instruments and a Volkswagen

Sardined up to the headliner in Dad's vintage Volkswagen,
lacking room enough to wedge in our juvenile jokes,
we steamed up the windows with hot, breathy laughter,
arms and legs intertwined, jammed against door hardware.

Our winter morning had earlier assumed a frantic edge,
when our school bus to all-district orchestra
failed to collect us as we clustered at our bus stop.

Seven young musicians clung to frosty strings and bows.

A panicked phone call to Dad, *mein Vati,* our transport wizard,
sent him to us Volkswagen in flight, its rubber band a whir.
He stacked us in with aplomb, a violinist on each side
of two cellists squeezed in the middle, petite violists on their laps.

Dad shouted, "One, two, three, small instruments on your heads,"
as he tenderly guided each through the window to its player.
Our bassist let out a guttural chuckle from the front seat,
face pressed immovably against his bass bag in a loving, bear hug,
while the headstock saluted all drivers and passengers,
poking out proudly from the quirky, medieval sunroof.

Whispers for a Future Self

Youth stood saucer-eyed peering
through the yawning door,
close enough to fill nostrils
with foreign fragrances
and be greeted by the soundtrack
of her future—
bold music infused with
euphony and cacophony.

She observed calmly, grappling
for the precise words necessary
to explain what had for hours
flashed before her.
Nuggets of wisdom to
explore unclaimed territory,
now presented the navigational
tools to chart her future.

She clutched the keys within
her perception at last,
after lingering at that door,
snatching clues and envisioning
through unique power,
secrets of encouragement,
of life, death, and beyond.

Then, she whispered all
ever so tacitly,
in my ear.

Traveling though Jasmine Nights

The squishy soles of worse-for-wear sneakers
were no match for the gravelly, spiky trail leading me
myriad times up the hill—a hill surely placed there to
torture me into shape and guide me like a personal
compass with alacrity through the jasmine-laden air—
to him.

In the undisturbed night when minds slumbered,
I peered out of my residence window to spot
the light slightly dimmed in his office signaling
me, enticing me into its beam, beckoning me to the
trail—as he waited.

The palpable hush cradled this traveler in the
divinely sensual perfume decanting from the night
blooming jasmine that masked everything painful,
as I, in dark solitude, held course along the pathway.

Those jasmine nights of yore transported me
from my youthful struggles to a forgiving world
where I could lose myself in another and breathe
in the life-affirming scent that each time
wrapped around my being and aroused me
to be open to possibilities.

Now and then, I detect a faint trace of jasmine
along my life's trail but never as fragrant as those
blooms that had once enveloped the pebbled path
leading me to peace—to bliss—to escape.

Contented I am with jasmine back then and never more,
those bushy, evergreen shrubs had defined my direction
with intoxicating directness that predicted risk—
evocative now are senses brimming with jasmine memories.

I walk the paved trail without the painfully steep hill,
fingertips brushing tenderly against perfect, waxy leaves
adorned by heady white flowers borne on—a calmly mild breeze.

A Toss of the Salad

Grandma's sylphlike fingers
caressed each leaf with kindness,
probing furrows and imperfections,
testing for crispness with tactile superpowers,
expertly tuned as perfection detectors.

Only the greenest of crunch she
tossed into the family's, garlic-saturated,
old Slavic, cherry wood bowl.

I stood mesmerized a thousand times
wedged in the narrow kitchen doorway,
a girl agog at the sight of
quiet elegance and steady poise,
admiration bursting from my heart
and love painting my soul.

She worked heedless of my teenage scrutiny,
head down tearing and mixing those
exotic, home-grown greens
I had learned to crave and savor,
then joined the leaves with
the darkest of succulent, crimson tomatoes,
color eclipsed only by her favorite lipstick.

I anticipated the final movement when
Grandmother tenderly grasped the wooden servers,
allowing the tangy dressing to lightly
kiss the top leaves while she began
to grab hold of the leafy gold
and ever so gently toss,
in contentment.

I attempted to remember each toss,
every ounce of technique,
the favorite positions of those ivory fingers.
But, most vividly I recall now the *mélange*
suspended in air when real time became irrelevant,
and she performed her grandmotherly magic.

The only sound between us
was servers skimming on wood.
Without turning around,
she asked me tenderly in Serbian to place
the family jewel on the table.

How did *moja baba* know?
She taught me her secrets.

Anxious I Was

Anxious I was . . . to see you—
      to re-trace the aura
      of your private place
      to climb peaks of fascination
      dominating within me
      to be entwined by the depth
      of your attention
      to yield to all desires between us.

Anxious I was . . . to see you—
      true, all of this,
        yet shy.

On the Road, Down the Road, Turn Off the Road

A far distance from the road to El Dorado,
a super, modern highway, or even
the yellow brick road,

the sinuous family road weathered by
potholes, fissures, and missed off-ramps,
appears twisted and rutted
as far as our collective eyes can detect.

We address the precarious stretch as *our lives,*
re-paved unendingly by our past, present, and future,
we live on that road existing year to year,
breathing, learning, loving, thriving, hurting.

We inch our way along in mortal quest,
toward enlightenment, acceptance,
and truth to continue on,
to pass on wisdom to those
traveling next in life's traffic.

Gathering up meaning from those
who have traveled before us,
in a different time and space,
we scatter messages behind
as clues to explain our presence.

We walk, dance, and slow down during our ride,
and stumble down the road,
confronting fellow travelers,
scraping ourselves up more times
than history can record,
protesting, demanding grace and honor.

Ignoring risks and threats,
educating ourselves in all things
familial, professional, useful or not,
we dubiously test every step with our toes,
hot, cold, lukewarm asphalt,
lying down in cooling plant beds,
sharing overpasses,
crouching warily in underpasses,
avoiding human error and accidents,
restoring our souls with rain and sunshine.

Dodging headlights, flashlights,
and streetlights glowing for us,
making U-turns we count signs,
cracks, miles and worn tires,
the hours whizz by and counting disappears,
ferrying us closer to the inevitable.

The destination creeps up on us,
without certainty of the approach,
we can see the sky, moon, sun and stars,
all is revealed at last as we
review our path on the final stretch,
laughing, crying, remembering the travels,
the years that defined our lives,
vividly recalling the best that melded with us,
the sky's dusky twilight cloaks us with forgiveness,
as we turn off the road.

To the Quiet Knoll

Muted thoughts telepathed between us,
as we cast down bleary eyes in respect,
encumbered by a reserve scored by years of footfalls
echoing on the worn tiled floors of our history.

Transcendence—no expression of actual words,
for we could vividly envision
from private years past, the collection
of heavy tears on the tips of mascaraed lashes.

 Mired down in unthinkable sorrow,
sounds of a country bleeding, trickling
off and pooling onto the sheet music below,
tear by solitary tear.

Creating a stain for all mankind, compromising
our joy in childhood, a song of mortality and eternal rest.
We hesitated for an instant as we climbed,
a channeling zephyr grazed our aged faces.

Mourning all over again the happening when our
lives were forever suspended in a void.
A waft of lavender roses snuggled
in our unsteady hands,

waiting to whither near the eternal flame,
a tribute to the man once beloved by the world.

We performed the music obediently in December,
flashes of notes ricocheted off the walls of recounting,
turning and glancing over one shoulder,
to hear the phantom piano not there.

In Paradisum sounded but for an instant,
then bore him safely away from relentless tragedy.

In Paradisum,
Deducant te Angeli.

Queen Tiye—Hound of Royalty

Created in svelteness,
swaddled in regal Egyptian colors,
hound of the hunt,
quiet talisman of the temples.

Enormous heart beating
to an ancient cadence,
gilded ages coursing through her veins,
love of the run,
eyes fixed forever keenly
on her prey.

Queen Tiye, our goddess,
bloodline of the ancients
walking in beauty and gentleness,
a perfect four-time gait.

Champion of the track,
and our hearts at home,
intelligence abounding,
dazzling, obsidian eyes
emanating affection and
life-sustaining love.

Providing uncut humor,
her long, slurpy tongue wraps
anteater-like around the
unsuspecting victim's fingers,
in solemn search of treats.

At repose upside down,
legs spread or paw gently
wrapped around her silly ear,
our gorgeous calendar girl,
nature's masterpiece of *dogness*.

Not for everybody,
attracting attention everywhere,
our forty-five mile per hour,
magnificent couch potato—
the hound of royalty.

Insistence, Persistence, and Resistance

Parents *insist* on flawless behavior.
Children rebel and turn centuries
of deaf ears to those words
that do not persuade,
becoming a chrysalis.

Words pupate, burst out,
emerging as mature thoughts.
At that juncture, we *insist*.

We *persist* during our drama
on the planet with ideas and
thoughts to convince the
worst of man's ignorance.

Shouting and protesting,
moving about in circles,
back and forth, to and fro.
At that point, they *persist*.

They *resist* the approaching change,
unwilling to cast away self-interest,
unsteady against the storm of doubt.
Buffeted by too many decisions.

Exhausted by crushing the songs of
the bearers of good tidings through
the millennia of attempts to formulate promises.
At that point, with that they *resist*.

Insist, persist, resist—actions learned,
but never internalized.

The Private Scaffold

Languidly, she removed the memento
from its velveted box.
Delicately dangling from
an intricately linked chain,
she clenched it in her hand aquiver.

So cold, she acknowledged the effect of
an otherwordly encounter likely to be relived,
to be experienced beyond any comparison.

Betrayed, she captured the warmth around her neck,
as it rested at home near the heart of her body.
Dormant until first light,
she craved the white remembrance again—
perhaps then or another day.

L.P.

The tall, stunning Siegfried of German linguistics
injected himself without fanfare into her student universe,
perfect vowels and mellifluous pronunciation abounding.

To steady focus on studies as demanded, was
seriously impossible from the moment of contact.
Scheiße—maddening yet calmly euphoric,
risky interludes,
the fast lane to the inevitable abyss of obsession.

With impaired, academic concentration,
limited further by sexual imaginings
and the occasional, late-night rendezvous,
linguistics emerged as her favorite subject.

The sheer beauty of the language—blinding,
all the rest, be damned.

An angelic, handsome looker to her, he was.
Easy, simply ignore the linguistic attributes!
With a tinge of strawberry locks, his look—
stylish compared to others in his wake.

Scattering trouble tempered with boyish charm,
he had a voice like Roman honey laced
with exquisite, French champagne.

And he loved champagne, she learned,
as *ihre Mutter* cleared
the cache of empty bottles
from her dorm closet at term's end,
with a sadistic scowl on her face and
I told you so in her eyes.

Caught—but stubbornly undeterred.

Mind Leaves

Leaves of thought clustering and whisking
through the arroyo of awareness in my mind.

Cradled in the wind of consciousness,
clumping onto the surface of knowledge.

Leaves of thought barricaded from the
limits of my thinking,

whirling and rushing,
ever and again gathering beneath the arroyo.

Leaves of thought gliding to meaning,
breaking open uncertainties,

lining the expanse.

A quiet kick into the leaves.

Light Sensations

A light flickers at my feet,
glowing, deathless warmth,
touched but unfelt.

A candle flame casts shadows,
formless,
reality marionettes,
there but unrecognized.

Heat masks pain,
sensation,
seeking refuge,
but only at my feet,
for

I must learn to perceive.

Time at its Beginning

The final celestial glimmer will take its
leave from the empyrean,

the ending tear will harden
on the cheek of destiny,

the earth will succumb to
dust's abraded hands,

the night will cease to open
the eyes of the fearful,

the dim glow will become the distant point
of all harkening,

and we will push ourselves on and on,

We, who seek renewal.

Life on the Hindenburg

The propaganda machine once captured hearts and minds.
Denial and horror—history provided the context of a hideous kind.

Brainwashed people accepted a one-way ticket to fly on the
  airship.
In modern times—impossible—grotesquely not.
Rotund, noisy, gaseous, explosive—the showpiece of the National
  Socialists,
lest the world should dare to forget the Swastika riveted on its
bloated tail.

Entombed in the past to reappear at a time when reason had died
and the world
stopped turning on its ancient axis, it emerged from the ghost
clouds where it
had soundlessly waited without purpose for years, muffled engines
revving
without a captain, awaiting mindless, tongueless passengers.

Circling the earth a thousand times over, aimlessly radiating evil
and
hate messages falling on heads and into the ears of all who
attempted to see
through the layers of thick clouds to decide for themselves,
what could be done to rescue the future of humanity from the
cataclysm at hand.

The flood of insanity drowned innocence, seeping into everyday
existence,
crushing kindness and integrity—the waiting to halt the airship
baffled
the world with minds pitted with fear, the indecency of the
approach

squeezed the life from the collective veins straining every day to see
colors in a bizarre black-and-white tragedy.

Four long years onlookers hurled rocks to stop the flight of
the gigantic blimp and mortally wound the captain.
The gas supply outlasted the sincerity of those lying in wait
daring to pounce, to get through to the truth and return
to safety on earth—no arms could reach that high.

The crash came without a burn but only at end of a term
with the return of thick clouds to cloak the airship and protect it
for later flights—shielded from the sun,
a dark, sinister bubble of life without eyes.

Apocalyptic.

Upon Hearing Barack's Words

Barack's noble words glided on the heavy air,
settling upon the chary listeners who were
barely present in a state of shock.

Past his time, the listeners had already realized
the political anguish seething beneath the
fissured plane of life in their homeland.

The listeners glanced at Barack
then at each other without words,
disintegrating inside with a withering
sense of hope, a commanding sense of national
doom, and wounded hearts at the loss before them.

Sorrow swallowed the air in the room.
The listeners wiped their eyes and nervously
shifted their weight in their chairs.
His mighty words were not enough
to medicate the pus-filled abscess of
civil war infecting the home front.

"It's still early," he said.
The listeners paused and
within eyeblinks, minds halted thoughts
of domestic death long
enough to break a smile and
imagine quiet possibilities.

But, he left the podium.
The lights dimmed along with
collective hope for a shred of
anything more promising to come.

Overcome with shame for
the country, themselves,
and for the future, the listeners
closed their eyes to face the peril.

A cavernous hole appeared
where political consciousness
once flourished.
Democracy collapsing.

Come, the Ravages

When crimson tempests,
violets blue,
yellow meadows,
fade into dull tones of obscurity,

the world will falter,
the people cease crying,
emotions turn to wordless silence.

Surrender to the ravages
of the invisible,
we convince ourselves.

Fateful Christmas Tree

Holiday-infused people beaming crooked smiles
frenetically trimmed a black Christmas tree,

until the tree sagged with ornaments and tinsel
and eventually frowned to the ground,
while the gifts lay strewn beneath.

A feeling no longer remaining
faded after the trimming,
as a small boy watched the reveries
with the tree towed away outside
by the garbage man.

Waiting for Mr. H

Shh . . . shh . . . shush!
What are you saying
strangely there muttering to yourself,
to your god?
How is your world—full of love?
Painless to shut me out, the non-believer.

Why aren't you yourself—who
stole you away from you?

Why do you continue talking?
Unbelievable, what nonsense!
Do you know what you are saying, man?
The repulsive change has come.
It didn't need to be.

You're gone, out somewhere.
Kiss your friend goodbye.
Quite easy to say for you, as
you can't hate—it's true, you know.

Why no reaction?
Waiting is victorious for us
who have passed on to you and to me.
Who is the loser—the god-awful of the couple?

Be solitary, god child,
don't sin and don't commit.
Hang on to numb ideas forever into pathos.

You, too, will learn to look back, someday.

Adieu, Blue Flower

Infinite, tiny laughter cascaded
into the garden of the future.

He plucked for her an elegant choice,
sweet, fleshy petals revealed stories
foreshadowing love.

A potent feeling emerged of merely
holding him in her heart,
budding silently as the flower,
opening only for him.

Come.
Dare walk with me in the garden.

You see, an old man comes.
Pluck a flower for him
to replace the blue one
that fell from his heart.

Please, come walk beside me.
It is our time.

A Matter of Seconds

Beings cravingly seek the rush,
the speed at which pedals hit the metal,
each day, every day hurling forward,
chasing daily drudges, gathering seconds
marinated in our encounters.

Faces leave imprints, books get written,
parents rear children who grow up and
develop opinions.
Talking, learning, and
laughing fill the earth's
murmuring with human sounds.

We recall those seconds when
life advances our moody reactions,
absorbed in our own thoughts,
but always together with humankind.

Discovering Howard Carter

Lee's boisterous school chums tripped over
themselves each day to reach the ball hut first to
grab the newest and plumpest balls for recess time.

She stuck faithfully to her recess routine,
remaining alone in the classroom spellbound
in silence, wonderstruck by another few, heavy
parchment pages from Howard Carter's book.

The spectacular book had astonished the world
for decades introducing the Egyptian boy King
from the 18th Dynasty.

Lee learned to pronounce the King's royal name,
Pharaoh Tutankhamun, which rolled off her
lips as smooth as the alabaster, canopic jars
which had preserved the Pharaoh's viscera,
devotedly wrapped and anointed with oils awaiting
reunion with the King in the afterlife.

Each, stunning page received Lee's adoring caress.
Some divulged an important piece of *the discovery*.
Some breathed life into elaborate drawings and notes.
Each reflected Dr. Carter's profound respect for the King.

Through the pages, Lee stepped into an ancient world.
She perceived firsthand opulence in gold, lapis lazuli,
carnelian, and obsidian swirling around her.
Her young, delicate fingers traced the contours—
of the Pharaoh's funerary mask.

The audible beat of her heart pulsated, her
breathing quickened as she cradled the scorching,
desert sand in her child's hand and felt its coarse
grit under her sandals of pounded gazelle
skin with soles of woven reeds.

Lee thanked Dr. Carter for acting as her quintessential
guide to all she had absorbed in those personal interludes,
savoring his exquisite details during recess.
Through his fierce, archaeologist's eyes Lee
wandered in the Valley of the Kings imagining him
at work in the tomb with flickering candle in hand,
as he peered through a tiny hole
in the entrance to the antechamber,
to behold *wonderful things*.

Continuance

Through all the worlds of weeping
into the broodiness of space,
through all the shades of gray forgetting,
and into the infinitesimal reaches of vision,

a person attempted to escape.

Surviving through courses of biting hatred,
and eventual rotting of goodness,
brushing all cares, wants and desires,
beauty, love, and departure, aside,

a person attempted to continue.

Friendship Rebounds

Summer's voice grew distant.
The faces were shadows
      of the recollections of yesterday.
      They had been here a while,
      truthfully, I convinced myself.

The suddenness caught my thinking on pause.
Temporality was out of focus
      for so long I had lived peace.
      As friendship came I realized,
      it had all passed.

Gone it was to be kept away
until another tomorrow was borne,
      on someone's smile.

The Adored Microwave

A lemon-filled, jelly donut
craved warmth each morning.
It waited patiently in the pink pastry
box amid sugary companions,
until the precise moment when
mein Vater would gently liberate
the selected, gooey delight from
the crowd to make it his early
meal.

One morning, the jelly donut made
a detour onto a large, glass plate in an
enormous metal box before it detected
my father's bite during the sacrifice.
Today was different, without a doubt.
A quick press of a red button
sent the pastry spinning in the box,
round and round, then, finally—
the heat arrived.

My dad admired his warm confection
with heightened anticipation,
before grasping it with two fingers,
placing it near the opened hatch.
He sighed and with adoration
thanked his colossal, new microwave
for the miracle of miracles—
a perfectly warmed donut in a minute.

Seduction by Darkness

Darkness seducing,
dripping from streetlights,
alighting everywhere,
hovering over the hush.

Graying stillness,
infusing and misty,
glinting iridescence,
sailing over skies.

Dampening crystals,
splashing fingers of grass,
crushing wet balconies,
leaning over the landscape.

Tell Me Your Name

I want to call you by name,
you the someone.
I could perish in your shadow,
only to whisper *no one*.

Until at last I would
grasp the perception that
kills all the emotion in
the center of your beliefs.

The cognizance that once
was with you,
now dies along with the
almost lover who halfly
sits here with me.

Heavy eyes with jaded love fading,
because a recourse in time beckons
my pledge on to an untimely end.

An end that must arrive to tell
us *both* your name at last.

Fleeing from Façades

What are these façades that people construct,
the laughing and smiling not their own.
Actions troubling others who fear to stay,
possessing words and concerns for themselves alone.
Creating a world of questions and false impressions,
distressing people who merely want to live unhindered,
these people strive for total, emotional demolition,

Nothing less.

It is from these walls of turmoil and loathing,
that I must flee.

Music Courses within Me

Cardiac rhythm beats through my heart,
Blood pounds with booming, resonant notes,
Nerves conduct electrical impulses,
Skin orgasms ripple through frisson,
The brain processes pitch and tone—
A sound system between my ears.

It is music in me.
Jazzy.
Symphonic.
New age.
Inspired.

Flattery Will Get You Nowhere

Nonchalantly, he poked his masterfully chiseled face
around the door frame like a suave periscope.

"Well, hello there, my beauty,"
escaped his lips aimed with fierce inflection.

Unsuspectingly, she swiveled her head and
positioned toward the tones of pure trouble.

Her eyes locked in with evil's Luciferian twin,
calmly wicked, murky, a deep cistern of mischief.

Her ears fell numb and for a fugitive lapse,
all other voices faded unable to penetrate.

"Don't answer," reverberated in her brain,
where reason and logic had long resided.

The awareness next hit—headed for the trap of traps,
condemnation to sweet misery.

Muted and super glued to the chair,
lead limbs waited for their worlds to collide.

The words streamed rapidly, one phrase upon another,
silky, amorous, daring elixir.

Sucked into the middle of a kaleidoscope,
creating a vortex of unmentionable desires.

Round and round whirred her thoughts seeking
an escape from what was about to be.

She held on tight, got a firm grip, and
hurled directly at him brazen-faced,
"Flattery will get you nowhere."

They Called Her Vesna

An arresting Slavic beauty, she floated among us,
    a bounty of wavy curls, flowing, liquid mahogany,
    encasing soulful, hazel-green eyes,
    emitting years of repressed, family pain,
    submerged to a depth no longer reachable
    by any goodness.

Old-world style was her totality, she despised and blamed,
    cold indifference for the mother tongue,
    hushed up among family members,
    with baggage borne in silence to their graves,
    no comfort to allay fears of generations,
    behind the mask of normalcy—she railed.

Fueled by seething bitterness, her music played on,
    while people sacrificed love at her altar,
    year after painful year offering no response,
    dead inside from wasted efforts to survive
    in a perpetual world of happy beings,
    haunted by everything and nothing.

Hidden secrets were too agonizing to reveal,
    even to those surrounding her with comfort,
    always driven to guilt and questionable intentions,
    with a compulsion to listen to stories of cruelty,
    when growing up with vile deeds unidentified,
    unutterable acts resulting in lasting scars.

A barren desert spit the sand of lost heritage,
    repressed anger directed at her children,
    attempting to find herself in the
    devastation smoldering inside,
    from ages of silent abuse at the
     hands of those who gave her life.

As kids, we attempted to understand,
       as the world ignored her problems,
       the pain, the invective, the hatred,
       and all the questions decaying inside,
       we suffered in silence and tried to love her,
       we dug in and followed our pursuits,
       avoiding our pitiful deaths by shame.

As adults, we sought emotional respite from personal ruin,
       then turned our backs at the right time,
       before it was too late for us,
       escaping into the half-light,
       rubbing our eyes to see the truth,
       we cast off the shackles of emotional divestment.

Mother Vesna died in the shadows without us,
       releasing decades of shattered hope and condemnation,
       to stop the lying and seething,
       nobody uttered a word,
       nobody heard the echoes of
       grandparents and great-grandparents—
       only vague notes of laughter,
       heralding the release to a future with whole light.

Brilliant Bliss

found happiness
with a somebody who
craves to be with
you to be unencumbered
in intellect and heart
to live within the
blinks of life
extending
into a future
of sentience and intimacy
of unshackled passion and
kindhearted faces and deep sighs
and bliss—and
all that is to forgive
and take together
as to respect in
unity in openness
and in peace—found
happiness with
a person who loves
to love to be gentle
and fearless and attempts
to show all emotions
to rid himself of
frustration and loneliness—
to venture to the heart and
core of the being to the
depths and come back
satisfied and tranquil as
long as his idea
remains within the soul.

Laughing, I Went in

I stumbled in laughing,
buoyant with every stride.
I sensed the hand of fate,
resided faithfully at my side.

But, the room was not friendly,
though I still made my descent.

I tried so hard, but
'twas all in vain.
So,
I came . . .
and went.

Stepping Past a Dream

The boy stepped past a dream,
vaguely glimpsing formless shapes,
eyes turning over smiles and ears weary
of untold words.

The boy attempted to catch a dream,
falling over hushed tones,
unfulfilled,
mind stumbling through ravines of
cramped aloneness.

Once the boy stared into the dream,
concrete future,
frightening madness.

Only a boy walking alone
in a vacuous world,
embracing darkness,
dancing with images,

he clearly saw himself, grinning.

Faces Full of Waves

OFF TO OUR BEACH—

Our sacred home away from home—*not far from home,*

The zig-zaggy coastline beckoned us alluringly at school—*like an undertow,*

An impatient wait for Easter break—*the surf was up—tubular, man,*

Lemon juice combed through perfect hair—*land mermaids with stingy bikinis,*

No earthly comparison to the sand between our toes—*itchy delight,*

Psychedelic beach towels on parade—*a life-sized checkerboard,*

Exposed body parts slathered with baby oil—*mayonnaise for the hard cores,*

Disappointingly overcast days—*the lobster burn was intensely worse,*

Squabbles over where to stash the radio—*acoustics improved by crashing surf,*

Crazy-good food abundantly stuffed into mouths—*no forgetting the orange potato salad,*

Body surfing the waves—*slamming the sandy bottom at the Wedge with steep sea walls,*

Berserk surfboarding at Huntington—*dangerous pilings drifting way too close,*

Body hydration to excess—*the invention of blind worship of the sun,*

Digging up and hurling primordial, sand crabs—*fresh clams abed in a seafood buffet,*

Hanging out in starry darkness in mixed company—*if you get the drift,*

Rapture in the sand was actually—*a bit gritty.*

We hit our beach again the next day . . . and the next . . . and the next . . . WAVES.

The Brightest Echo

Lighted silence overshadows
      shining dimness,
        sighing peacefully,

Voices rising
      shouts of excitement,
      emotions abounding,

Reaching out
      carefully projected,
      to seize the brightest echo.

Sky Children of Nature

two and three million soarers
rounding,
merging with the air,
glissading through cumulus clouds,

tiny, fleeting spirits.

dimly visible they fly
come and leave,
lending their lives to
shadows in the sky.

o listen, you free, majestic bodies,
you who are flying,
creating patches of muted beauty.

take me up to
your celestial life,
surround me with your freedom,
beyond any apologies,
you sky children of nature.

Persistent Love

Persistent love—ardent desires,
Acting without knowing.
Composing the heart's unfinished concerto.

Persistent love—exalted yearnings,
laughing and grieving.
Melding two spirits
through imperfect lifetimes.

Persistent love,
souls intensely surrounded,
with essence tumbling.
Two people seek other answers
within their realities.

Persistent love,
Spoiling and fading.
I captured a buried meaning,

An insistent fire
in place of my strength.
Persistent love itself—
clinging to bravery.

The Flavor of Cold

Take the rain away.
Pocket the wet quietness.
Drink up the cold flavor.
Hide it for another day.

Are We the Dizzy Intruders?

Dizzy, so very dizzy.
The constellations struggle
to spell beauty across the sky.
The fog creeps into our eyes as the
muffled sounds of the world resound off the
walls of nature's boundary.

Outside, we are aware of passing cars
but connect with the comfort here inside.
Safely nested away from the wet noise,
to hear the ship's whistle but
again see the eternal flame burning below.
Touched by warmth so distant inside,
though not here with us.

Surrounded by edges of green giants,
hurdling over endless mountains with
fat, ripe berries.
The leaves look down on us,
here as intruders.

We are here alone to harm no one,
not even the red fox.

An Autumn Reality

When we finally awoke into materiality
and perceived that we had lost those times
we can now only vaguely remember,
it was too late for promises,
for everyone was near regret.

We all had to leave.

Had to push on to our own journeys,
to emerge again with different faces

when autumn arrived.

Elusion

Why ask anybody about *him?*
You are selfish and don't wish him happy.
It is only your satisfaction to pass on to the next pilgrimage,
to the next absurdity that leads only to blind resentment
and impotent actions that cannot be expressed.

Because god, the giver and keeper of the light,
says it's wrong, illuminating no lightlessness,
yet you have no answers in your own quiver.

The demons have been cast out to the sea of sinful
emotions you believed you once directed
to him, now cowering within you,
an internal, personal rebellion of forces.

It distresses me to think about what you see
of his world, you exist, yet no one acknowledges
you are present—there are only impassive spaces,
not yet filled with substance—
with tiny shards of attempts of abiding forgiveness.

Your eyes swing to the rhythm of hymns.
You stone him with your hypocritical tongue.
You preach brotherhood and kindness—
Observe, it is you who is stony and cruel.

You give your life over to fairy tales on incalculable faith.
Whom will you love? Whom can you love
in your state of faithful sightlessness?
You only tolerate the deception,
the things you cannot concretize but thrive on.

You have gambled away his old identity,
for a new, anonymous countenance
that has crushed *you*—the master elusionist.

Andersch's Cherries of Freedom

The wild cherry tree enticed Alfred with *Kirschen der Freiheit,*
Andersch's precise words capturing the seconds in which
he chose desertion from the crushing, last gasps of the fascist
drama that had stalked him like an obscene, sinister shadow,
inching closer to defeat him during the Italian campaign.

Without protest, he had endured his father's return from the
Great War, a shell-shocked, disillusioned nationalist, broken
inside and out, wounds putrefying and unable to cope with
the remains of the corpse he called his homeland—
incoherent rantings about his *Deutschland* and the
collapse of the Weimar Republic and the Nazi ascent.

His handwritten pages slid easily from the tattered
archival box conferring protection for many years.
I beheld the small, timid script of the reticent author who
had selflessly promoted young, unknown writers and joined in
to re-establish the broken traditions of German literature
post-World War II, as a tribute to building democracy.

I leafed through his writing with heavy, weepy eyes
intellectually entranced by the vibrations of a determined soul
using his pen to capture some meaning from then to his present,
applying his re-education by American military to
introduce compromise and pave a road to democracy.

He picked a handful of the *deserter's cherries* while
The *Panzer* unit rolled away muted in the distance,
a game of cat and mouse with the Americans in pursuit.
Andersch thought about how the tanks should wait as
time belonged to *him* only as long as he ate the cherries.

They were light red and glassy—he *freely* ate another handful.
Reverently, I sat and read, contemplating the works Andersch had
contributed without the fame of Grass, Böll, or Kästner.
No Nobel Prize for Andersch. . .
only the euphoria from his minutes of personal freedom.

Effects from Endless Peaches

Elation tapped me on the shoulder when I grew tall enough
to reach the tree boughs without my rickety chair.
I had always gazed up at them as the sun
filtered through and around the leaves,
trickling sunlight on my face and hair alight,
barely able to see the objects of my desire—*the peaches.*

It was my grandfather's tree, *mi abuelo,* who trimmed,
and fussed, and watered, and admired from afar,
the very lifeline for the fruit that seemed to grow
even during the winter,
as I remembered all those bittersweet years later.

I picked and lightly rubbed the abundantly hirsute gems
on my cheeks with longing teeth penetrating the downy skin,
leaving a bitter taste to protect the delicate, creamy meat,
that to me possessed a series of tasty jolts unsurpassed
by anything earthly to which I could compare his fruit.

The seasons came and went with pruning in between.
The peaches flourished under the envious eyes of resident birds.
The silky juice continued to dribble down my chin onto my arm,
down to my fingertips creating pools of aromatic, sticky honesty.
I considered this all to be my sublime indulgence.

The pies, the ice cream, and the delicate pastries followed,
a transformation of fruity matter into edible artistry.

I accepted the gastronomic changes without complaint.
Every bite and spoonful retained their original, divine flavor.
My world remained tinted with a peach-colored under glow,
enhanced with a subtle aftertaste of Gramps' own sunshine.

Blue Tunnels

I lament not always having revered my universe
and myself within it during melancholic interruptions,
life's interstitial spaces *sans* sense and portals,
leading to any sanguine illumination—
no heartening choices for quiet repose.

Detained in my own head by life's trials,
catching myself adrift in a chasm defined
by dense walls of layers of grief,
impenetrable by my own or other voices,
there existed only blue tunnels without atmosphere,
choking and distorting daily existence.

Exits appeared and led me out of the blue,
welcomed times of clarity and solace,
life renewed at an elemental level.

Reflections on Heritage

Who has not surveyed their maturing face
in the bathroom mirror,
the tell-all instrument of truth and torture,
day after day, every day,
every creviced wrinkle, it seems.

I've peered back at my countenance
in quiet condemnation of
those dark circled eyes,
lids beginning to droop,
cheeks begging mercilessly for collagen.

I have assured,"'Tis only a distorted reflection,"
while I startled myself with
discernable whimpers and groans,
wringing my chapped hands,
tongue protruding between bared teeth.

Overcome by an unattractive version of me,
a bolt of reality strikes exposing memory,
a swift recalling of personal history,
a calming of the instant desperation,
I see through the reflection to the core.

My own core created by my DNA history,
organized exclusively within my chromosomes,
tiny voices embedded in all I do,
cellular messages with genetic directions from
family contributors spanning our cosmos.

Tears breathlessly fall and blur my image,
the temporal vastness veils all negatives,
rescuing me from my ugly, grey funk,
illuminating the unique heritage encased within me.

Speaking with Eyes

In a subtle way, that day you were separate.
Your eyes spoke messages
I did not comprehend.

Thoughts of loving you crazy,
Attempted to help me see through your eyes.
They did not comprehend.

I could not speak any secret words,
Confusion caught me mute and absent.
My mind did not comprehend.

All that came before, reflected in my eyes,
Shooting past like a player—
My part I did not comprehend.

You were leaving . . . I realized.
Even then, your eyes spoke messages
I would never comprehend.

Dew on the Slug

Inhumed in law studies on a darkly somber, early morn,
weighed down by tediousness and pallets of stress,
I seriously considered another gargantuan-sized pot of coffee,
as fatigue lurked fiber-deep in each cell of my body.

In survival mode, seeking even the tiniest of distractions
necessary to avoid the sinkhole where aspiring lawyers go to perish,
I reached for the coffee, a filter, and my favorite, big-mouth mug,
as the drip, drip, drip provided a flashback to the last contracts lecture.

Awaiting the fix from my raspberry chocolate cup of joe,
craving attention from my snoozing fur children,
I unsuccessfully attempted to rouse them to play,
then averted my gaze avoiding contact with sleepy hound eyes.
Seduced by the idea of purging stale thoughts with freshly chilled air,
the screen door to the patio noiselessly swung open,
presenting the slick, wooden deck beckoning me to step out,
as I escaped clutching my cup and steadying myself near our hungry trash can.

Twisting around to reach the porch light switch—the casting of eerie particles,
the spotted slug bathed in diffused light appeared in the corner of my eye,
I hovered then stared downward at the magnificent mollusk,
waves of contraction and relaxation, traveling with antennae aflutter.

Soft tickles as antennae made contact with one palm, then the other,
allowing me to run my index finger gently along his slender back,
I drew deep breaths while my finger accompanied him across the plastic lid,
so powerfully fragile, alert at the dawn of the day—cloaked in *dew.*

It was back to the books with renewed concentration,
another cup of coffee and a pat on furry skulls,
impressed by observing nothing *slug-ish* about my *dewy slug,*
and that during my studies, *I* had epitomized the vernacular—
common slug.

I had taken part in my private *slug fest* that morn—
the next day my *dewy slug* was gone.

A Gathering of those Old Sayings

Side-by-side through generations,
we endured,
those old familiar sayings,
embedded in our collective consciousness,
humanely guiding us along—

a bucket-load they go.

A penny saved is a penny earned,
Don't count your chickens until they've hatched,
The squeaky wheel gets the grease,
Beauty is in the eye of the beholder,
A stitch in time saves nine . . .

Memorized them all—'til they became mine.

Don't put your eggs in one basket,
Blood is thicker than water,
It's raining cats and dogs,
Don't look a gift horse in the mouth,
The walls have ears . . .

Repeated them earnestly—over the years.

It's a piece of cake,
Bite the bullet,
Bury the hatchet,
Kill two birds with one stone,
Turn a blind eye . . .

Shared with generations—a cultural sigh.

Barking up the wrong tree,
You are never too old to learn,
Mad as a hatter,
When pigs fly,
Break the ice . . .

Wove them into public discourse—as language spice.

Look before you leap,
On thin ice,
Cat got your tongue,
You are what you eat,
Live and learn . . .

Labeled and indexed—to easily discern.

A chain is only as strong as its weakest link,
A dog is man's best friend,
A fool and his money are soon parted,
You can't get blood out of a turnip,
That is beating a dead horse . . .

Employed them throughout life—as a natural force.

Waiting for the Exact Hour

The malaise—it is there, skulking,
whispering hesitant salutations to dozens
of interludes, hundreds of expressions
meaning *you,* throughout the coupling.

The emptiness—it is greater than silent visitors,
non-reality,
slipping into those zones where feelings
at one time fell open into
life, changing yet still within
your grip.

The unbelievable—it is tap dancing
through your mind, ambivalence,
reflecting a true paradox
of a past and a future,
a silent stream losing finite motion.

The acceptance—it exists in
all of this and even more beyond,
within the endurance of a corner
in space, evolving onto a
plane where perhaps
perceptions and truths return back home.

The person—he is also there,
living behind the complex of confusion
and reactions—waiting,
gathering strength to decide,
when the exact hour arrives
to reveal the beauty that
is he.

Look to the Vastness not Yesterday's Hurt

No use to weep for youth
Lamentation cannot wash away longing
Age at last bringing gifts
Look to the vastness which
Tells us to grow up and
Search for words and
Meanings in the era
Of our lives which seem
To have perished without motive.

Uncovering new truths in
The ways we present ourselves
Allowing select ones to work closely
With us in defining something
We cannot reach alone forever
It is upon us you and me
The destiny that finally claims
Our minds and grows
Into old footprints leaving mature cracks.

It is right to give me yourself
I cannot tell you where we go
We will succeed far beyond our own images
We will grow tired yet not pause
For hesitation cannot exist in
This age which is meant
For us to progress into future energy
Brushing aside invention and all
That had hurt us yesterday.

Not Impressed by his French Kiss

Imagine: parked in a strange driveway in my new, red hot Chevy, contemplating life as I knew it at the moment.
Nervously, I waited to catch a discrete glance at the Adonis
I hardly knew but had schemed on during each rehearsal.

My body ensconced in the snug, bucket seat oozed casual sexiness.
While perfume molecules struggled to escape through the slim window crack,
I asked myself if I should bravely go inside or play it cool.
I compromised and rolled down the window.

Seen or be seen repeated itself as a constant refrain in my head, as I dawdled.

The steering wheel put up no resistance, as I gripped it with sweaty, white knuckles,
sliding both hands side to side around the classic, pleather cover.

Glancing furtively in the rearview mirror in case he left the party by the side door,
I elevated my eyes, blinked, and there he stood leaning on the long, sleek hood.

My James Dean brushed two perfect fingers tickling gently along the Chevy's curves,
gliding as he moved in slo-mo still in stage make-up and costume.
Framing his perfect physique in starry, stygian blue was the summer sky.
I turned my head just as he tilted his and leaned in with readied lip missiles.

Oh shit, this could be it, I thought, aware of the blush.
Our lips became a quiet duet, a lovesick coming together gathering momentum,
moist impact with a pleasant firmness,
until his corpulent tongue thrust in, worming down my throat.

I sighed, wiped away the slobber, and drove off.

Where I Rest

It was an effortless ascent,
scaling up the mount,
where I serenely discovered,
what I had often sought.

It was all I had longed for,
Lucid images a mystical
force had brought.

I found enduring quietude,
and I found unending rest.
If only it could have been infinity,
on that glacial, mountain crest.

A Girl on Standby

A girl stood by silently,
inside crying,
destroying,
tearing apart the corners of dank meanings.

A girl stood by silently,
inside hurting,
fading,
pulling the inner strings of a
background of naive memories.

A girl stood by silently,
inside burning,
ceasing,
folding to ages of shredded,
confused ambitions.

A girl stood by silently,
inside crying,
thinking,
outwardly motionless,
she stood,
silently happy.

Silent Shroud

A shadow beneath her timorous smile,
moist eyes of youthful introspection,
buried in thoughts of reluctance and fear,
searching for a life
behind a cognizable meaning.

Pain from years when life was savage,
a line blurred between reality and truth,
obscure tones of wanted bits of cares,
confused ends of unwanted
tangles of dreams.

Little girl being, pictured as a part
of this world,
casting thoughts of
only uncolored substance,
drifting to locate a piece
of unfelt happiness.
Forlorn but bold,

a silent shroud of goodness.

Winter Anew

Polar-bear freezing here we experience
ice sickle-ish, biting days,
days of lingering smiles,
numb lips and
forgotten frowns.

Children days,
days of endless pranks and
snowy foothills.

Window days,
days of curious noses pressed against the panes,
and feeling only inside warmth and spirit.

Sparkling days,
days of real living and
home fires blazing on
the hearths of young souls.

Rainy Life Tears

Fleecy rain sashayed from a distance,
tickling the earth like fingertip tears.

In low tones, rose perfection broke
through the earth unaided,
drops descended and
nuzzled its petaled face . . .
tears of growth,
Life altering.

Somewhere, a person lay mute,
two raindrops fell and unparched
the restrained lips . . .
Rain tears, givers of anticipation.

I roamed alone to meet somebody.
Two tears melted from somebody's eyes,
onto my cheek . . .
Tiny raindrops of you.

Angles of Love

Love me now, I beseech you.
Present is our now,
present is living,
and we are alive.

Love me absolutely, I beg you.
Perfectly is our absolutely,
perfectly is our always,
and you are my future.

Love me honestly, please.
Honestly remains unquestioned,
and unquestioned is our devotion,

and devotion,
irresistibly is.

In Love with Love

Ambushed by the endless cycle of seeking love in life,
waves rolling in and beaching themselves on the shore unendingly.
Driven to crave more and more,
until we no longer recognize ourselves, *in love*.
Pavlov's dogs—no denying the fate.
The head rush like potent drugs masks our intentions to the point
of losing ourselves.
Is it I, or is it he or she, we ask?
We cannot determine the difference at some opaque point in the
cycle.

An enraptured heart beats and urges us forward beyond rational
decisions.
Caught in the spider's web, *Huis Clos,* as Sartre informed us.
But we persist in the adrenalin-driven hunt
culminating in a match made in heaven,
or a stay dead-ending within the penumbral corners of purgatory.

Who has traveled there?
Who still migrates there?
Enjoy the romp,
we love-savoring beings.

Fantasy of Fantasies

What a fantasy I dwell on.
Within my lover's reach,
I am capable of expressing
in speechless words what now
has invaded my mute spirit.

My complete being awakens
piqued by even your never touch,
and accepts the love trembles
like a delicate bird in hand,
hidden only for us.

I am able to gracefully imagine the
flavoring of our inexhaustible realm
with the brilliance of our nexus,
the veil of adulation, the silhouette of the sun,
living unfettered within us.

I savor earthly rapture in realizing
I could awake in a latitude to come
to you enabled in our truth,
to tell you what erupts inside me now.
What a fantasy I have from affection to ardor.

Death of the Top Hat

Perceived through a child's eyes,
the immediate present claimed her future.
Unrevealed at the moment, images in black
and white appeared in real-time
on a television screen—
the magical, looking glass.
Silent waiting began to an end of hope.

The child watched the tall, handsome man
dressed to the nines on a chilly, January day,
top hat in place,
smile to a crowd—a country that needed him,
wanted him, and believed in him.
His beautiful wife stood close by,
aglow with admiration,
too stunning for such youthful comprehension.

The child listened as Robert Frost read,
top hat in place,
splendid words for her young ears.
Her reading of his poems in school paled to
seeing and hearing him on the television.
The poet made mistakes and faltered,
but he read on, and the child
closed her eyes to concentrate better.
She wept.

The child saw breath draped in the winter air
and thought how difficult it must be to speak
in frigid weather as she sat snug in front of
the television on a warm, California, January day.
People wore bearish coats, though, she mused.
It could not be too uncomfortable as long as
things did not drag on and on.

In the cramped living room, the child sat transfixed with
family all around, smiling and pointing at the television
whenever a famous person appeared.
There were many, famous people that day,
too many to count anyway.
The child had only heard their names—
no internalization at that point in time.
That is, except for President Eisenhower,
who had been the child's President until that day.
The two looked so very different together,
weighted down by January's cold mantle.
He appeared happy for the tall, handsome man,
powerfully shaking his hand while
he looked deeply into his eyes,
nodded, and passed on unshared secrets
the child would never know anything about.

The child's family spoke with admiration about Ike,
high praise for work after the war,
peace and healing they said with cracking voices.
The child did not know about that either
but kept watching until the tall, handsome man
spoke with an accent not like her family's.
What was it, she wondered?

The room slipped into silence with the gathered crowd on the television.
The child felt brushed by greatness as the man continued to speak
with words that penetrated deeply that day,
to be remembered years later by almost everyone.
How could that be, the child was to ask at some
unidentified time in the future when the realization would hit her—
an unspeakable event had cheated her altered universe.

The child felt something shift that icebound, January day
within her *Weltanschauung* no longer restricted—
she became part of the modern world with much
promise and confidence approaching in her life.

She observed the tall, handsome man,
the new President, standing confidently
and proudly beaming at everyone at the exact time
a shadow fell over him for a split second.
What was that the child asked her family?
Did you see it?

Nobody seemed to know.
Nobody answered her.

The child became aware of the annoying ticking
of her grandmother's old country clock—
so loud, wresting everyone back into the realities of the day.
Somewhere, in anticipation though, another clock ticked in
the murkiness with the alarm set for a much sadder day.

Windows for Choosing

Barely visible before me there,
two windows, two choices.
Rippling, faintly shimmering,
shallow on the water's surface.

Two opportunities to float along
the wavy passages of my corporality.
A vision, now blinded from the
images of time—
hallowing, spiritedly looking for exits.

Two windows, either unique,
both exotic and precarious.
Undulating shadows seeking form,
lest I choose.

But, which? Dare I look?

I ask—which is my courage?

Purple Salve

I lack exact recall of *the* moment in which
the world harmonized face-to-face with purple,
when everything yielded to all of the
permutations of those adored shades of nature,
a union of incredible forces.

The rapture came slowly you see,
creeping in with lavender and deep, smoky tones,
regal, yet at times shy and pouty, or understated,
in phases unremarkable until gentler eyes
journeyed across the earth's landscape,
vision sharpened in the quiet afterglow
of the desert sky's hues.

A purple salve created a soft layer,
with exquisitely warm fingers to caress,
and calm the noise of life,
a luminous performance,
a reckoning of space and dimension.

Behold the color of immortal lenses,
a catalyst of what is to be.

About the Author

Born in Los Angeles, novelist and poet Janice L. Smith-Hill, writing as Lee Orlich Bertram, earned her BA, MA, and PhD at the University of California, Irvine. After a successful career in K-12 public education as a teacher and administrator, she earned her JD at the University of Idaho and began the practice of law in the states of Idaho and Washington. In addition to her law practice, Lee teaches business law and the law of international trade at Washington State University. She is multilingual, hails from an immigrant family, is well-traveled, and enjoys reading, sitting on corporate boards of directors, archaeology and Egyptology, and playing her piano. Lee's *nom de plume* honors both sides of her family.

Insistence, Persistence, and Resistance is Lee's debut collection of poetry and includes selections reflecting a lifetime of deeply personal observations about and reactions to the highs and lows, individuals, and events that have greatly impacted her life.

Lee currently makes her home in Idaho with her husband of many years, Dr. Jack Hill, and their feather and fur children.

www.ingramcontent.com/pod-product-compliance
Lightning Source LLC
Chambersburg PA
CBHW031201160426
43193CB00008B/460